LET'S DRAW DINOSAURS AND PREHISTORIC BEASTS WITH CRAYOLA!

ILLUSTRATED BY BRENDAN KEARNEY

LERNER PUBLICATIONS ◆ MINNEAPOLIS

Official Licensed Product
Lerner Publications Company
A division of Lerner Publishing Group, Inc.
241 First Avenue North
Minneapolis, MN 55401 USA

For reading levels and more information, look up this title at www.lernerbooks.com.

Main body text set in Billy Infant Regular 24/30.
Typeface provided by SparkyType.

Library of Congress Cataloging-in-Publication Data

Names: Kearney, Brendan (Illustrator), illustrator.
Title: Let's draw dinosaurs and prehistoric beasts with Crayola! / illustrated by Brendan Kearney.
Description: Minneapolis : Lerner Publications, 2019. | Series: Let's draw with Crayola! | Includes bibliographical references. | Audience: Ages 4–9. | Audience: K to Grade 3.
Identifiers: LCCN 2017061741 (print) | LCCN 2018015967 (ebook) | ISBN 9781541512542 (eb pdf) | ISBN 9781541511026 (lb : alk. paper)
Subjects: LCSH: Dinosaurs in art—Juvenile literature. | Prehistoric animals in art—Juvenile literature. | Drawing—Technique—Juvenile literature.
Classification: LCC NC780.5 (ebook) | LCC NC780.5 .L48 2019 (print) | DDC 704.9/4329—dc23

LC record available at https://lccn.loc.gov/2017061741

Manufactured in the United States of America
1-43986-34000-6/27/2018

CONTENTS

CAN YOU DRAW DINOSAURS
AND OTHER PREHISTORIC ANIMALS?

You can if you can draw shapes! Use the shapes in the box at the top of each page to draw the bug or critter parts. Put the parts together in your drawing to make a spiky stegosaurus or a ferocious *Tyrannosaurus rex*. Or use the parts to make your own dinosaur!

DINOSAUR AND PREHISTORIC ANIMAL PARTS

Shapes you will use:

circle   rectangle   triangle   half circle   oval

Eyes

Arms

Wings

Legs

Tails

Tyrannosaurus rex

Spinosaurus

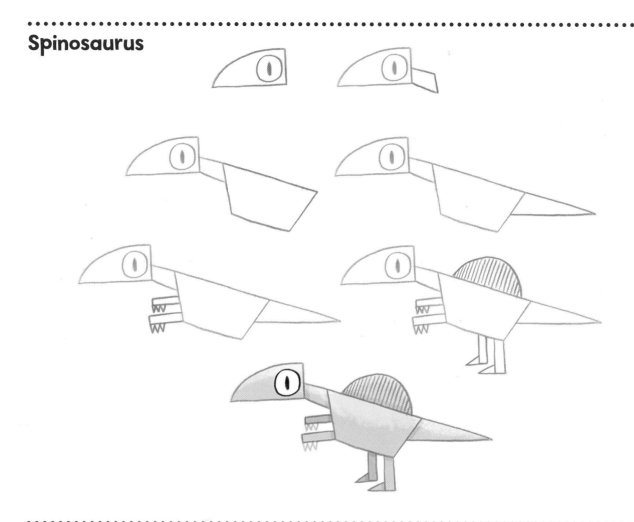

Velociraptor

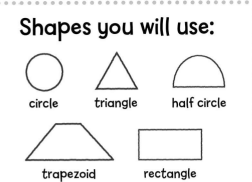

Shapes you will use:

circle triangle half circle

trapezoid rectangle

Megaraptor

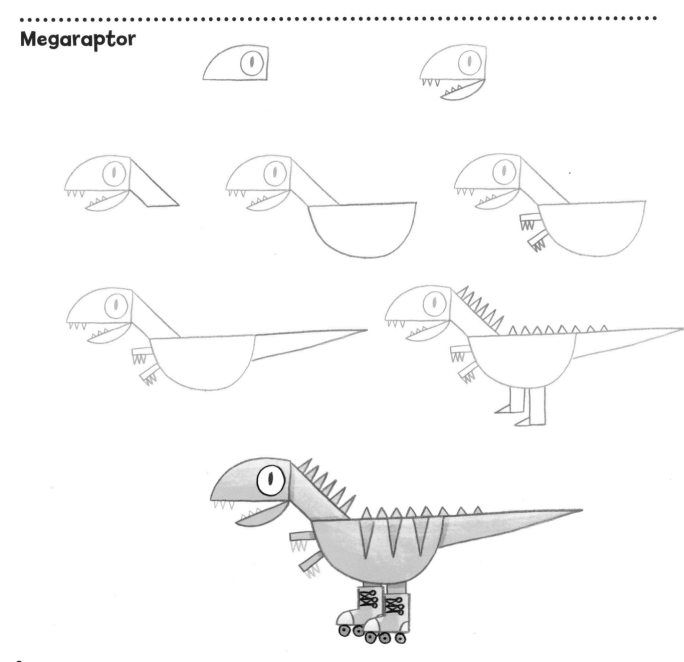

Oviraptor

I eat plants too!

Giganotosaurus

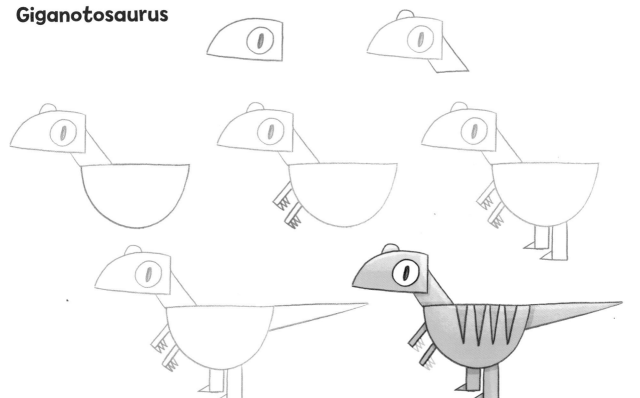

9

Shapes you will use:

circle — half circle

triangle — rectangle

Brachiosaurus

Triceratops

Hadrosaurus

11

Shapes you will use:

circle   triangle   half circle

rectangle   oval

Diplodocus

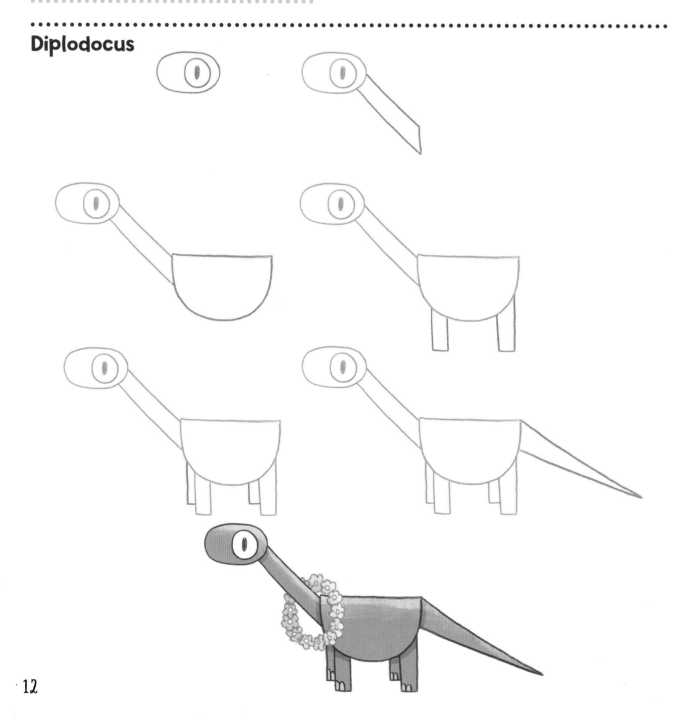

Iguanodon

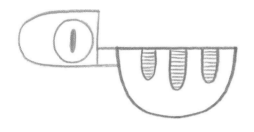 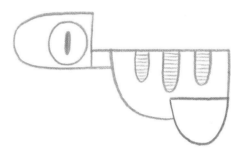

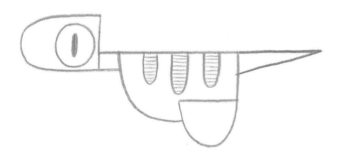 

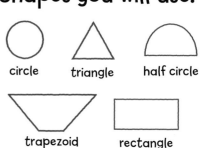
Elasmosaurus

14

Pliosaurus

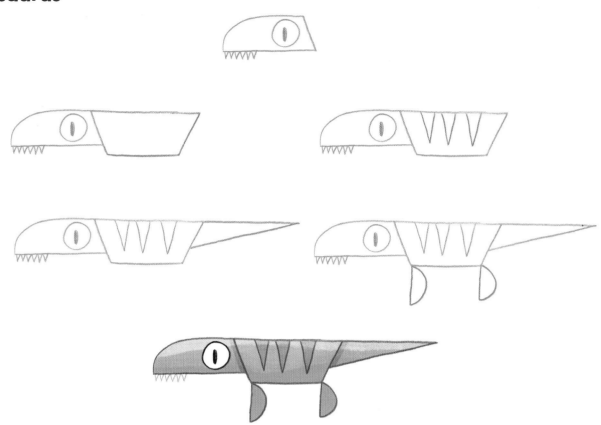

Tylosaurus

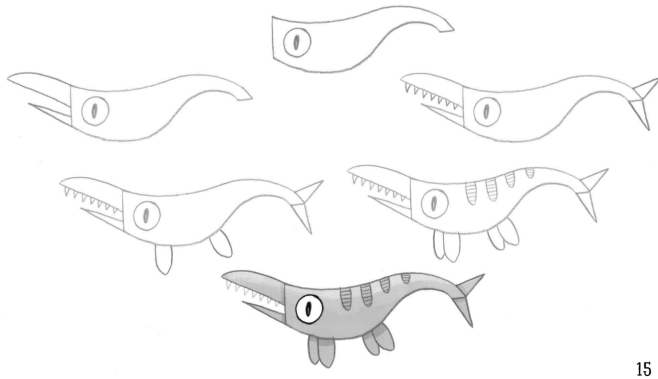

FLYING DINOSAURS

Shapes you will use:

 circle triangle half circle rectangle

Pteranodon

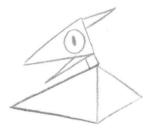 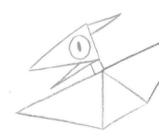 

Quetzalcoatlus

 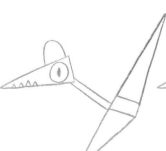 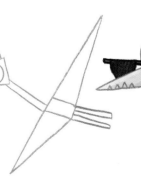 

16

Microraptor

Pterodactyl

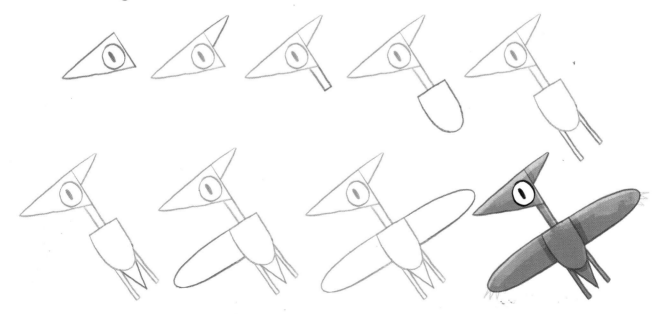

17

Shapes you will use:

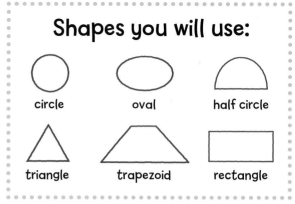

circle · oval · half circle

triangle · trapezoid · rectangle

Stegosaurus

Sauropelta

Ankylosaurus

19

FUNNY-LOOKING DINOSAURS

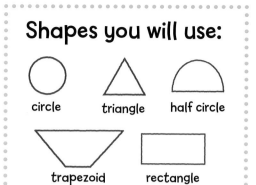
Stegoceras

Suzhousaurus

Longisquama

21

MADE-UP
DINOSAURS

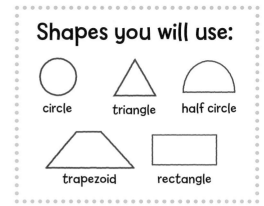

Shapes you will use:

circle triangle half circle

trapezoid rectangle

Flying Fangodon

Helmetasaurus

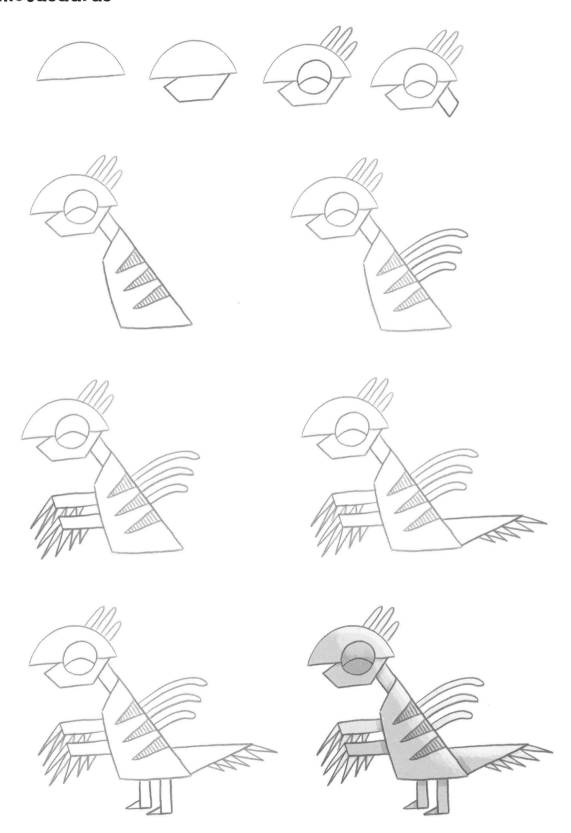

DINOSAUR MASH-UPS

Hasmosaurus

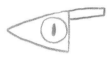

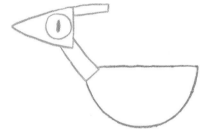

Tristegobrachus

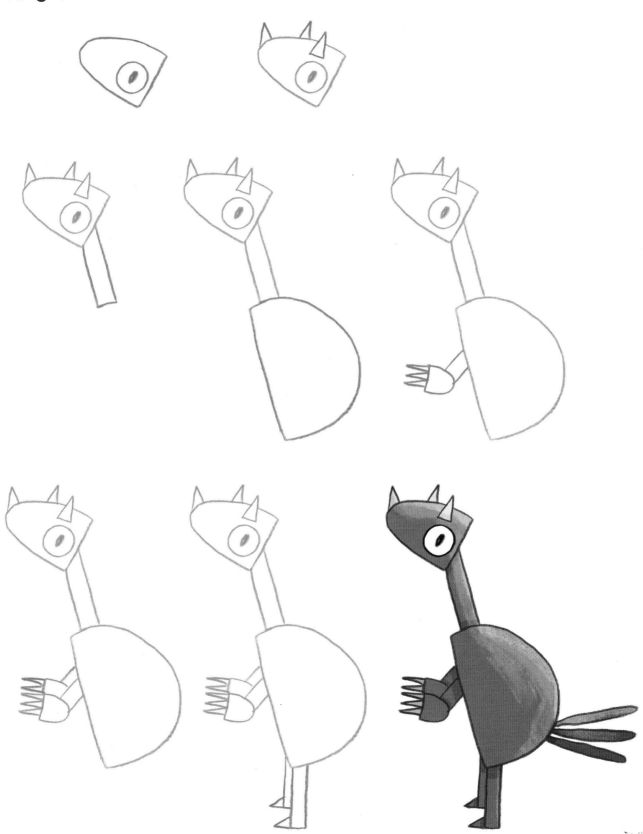

OTHER
PREHISTORIC
BEASTS

Shapes you will use:

○ circle △ triangle ⌒ half circle ▭ rectangle

Woolly Mammoth

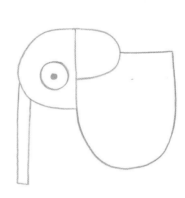

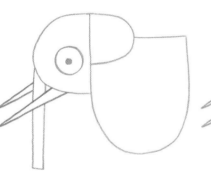

26

Saber-Toothed Cat

Short-Faced Bear

27

DINO DAY OUT

WORLD OF COLORS

Colors are all around us! Here are some of the Crayola® crayon colors used in this book. What colors will you use to draw your next dinosaur?

PEACH

CHESTNUT

BURNT SIENNA

MAHOGANY

MAUVELOUS

BRICK RED

RED

SUNGLOW

BANANA MANIA

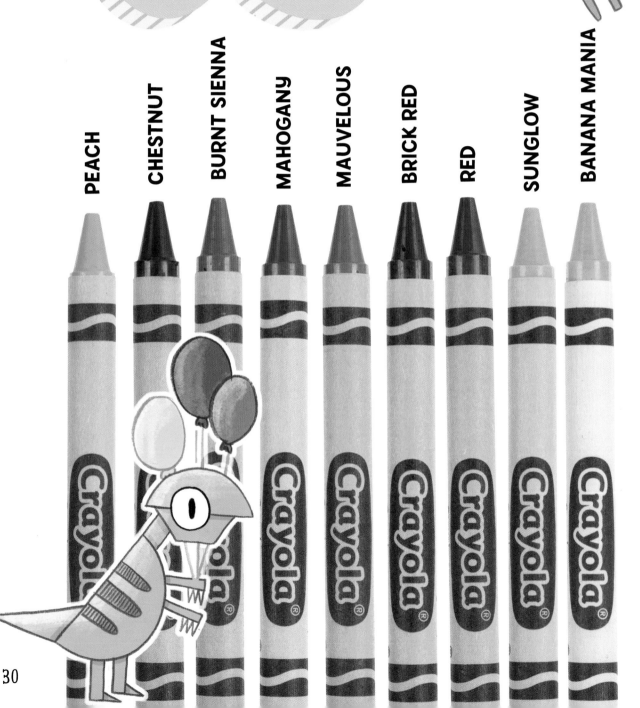

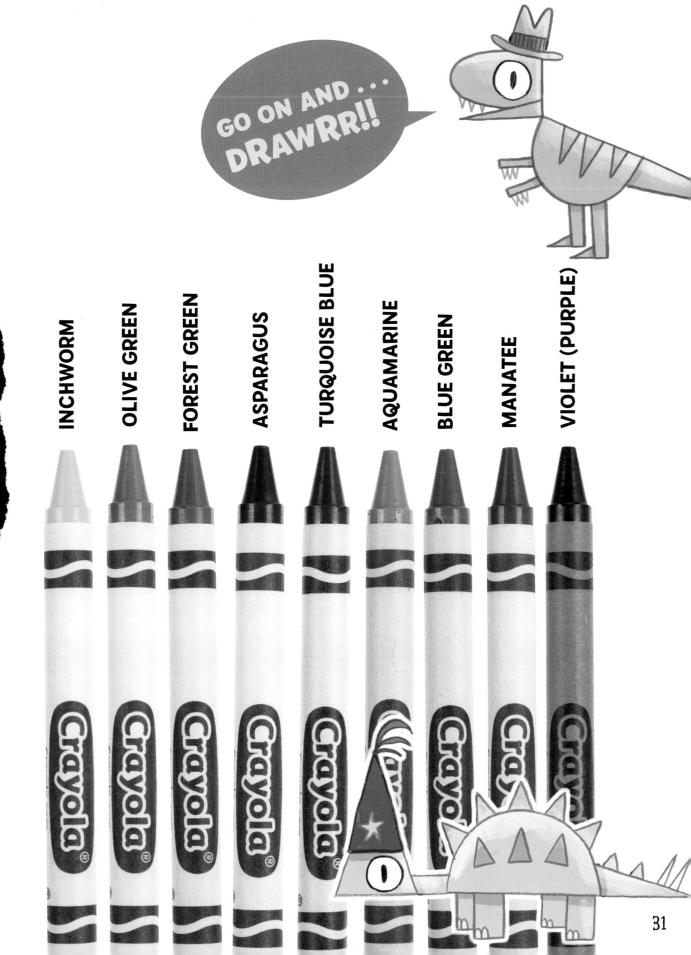

31

TO LEARN MORE

Books

Bergin, Mark. *It's Fun to Draw Dinosaurs and Other Prehistoric Creatures*. New York: Sky Pony, 2011. Follow the step-by-step instructions to learn how to draw more dinosaurs.

Brecke, Nicole. *Dinosaurs and Other Prehistoric Creatures You Can Draw*. Minneapolis: Millbrook Press, 2010. Look at this book to get more practice drawing your favorite dinosaurs and other prehistoric animals.

Legendre, Philippe. *I Can Draw! Dinosaurs, Dragons & Prehistoric Creatures*. Irvine, CA: Walter Foster, 2015. Check out this book to draw creatures such as dinosaurs, dragons, and more.

Websites

Dinosaur Diorama
http://www.crayola.com/crafts/dinosaur-diorama-craft/
Give your dinosaur illustrations a cool backdrop by creating this dinosaur diorama.

How to Draw Dinosaurs
http://www.hellokids.com/r_574/drawing-for-kids/drawing-lessons-for-kids/how-to-draw-dinosaurs
Visit this website to learn how to draw more of your favorite dinosaurs.